St Lucia

The Official Travel Guide

© Copyright 2017 by _____ - All rights reserved.

This document is geared towards providing exact and reliable information in regards to the topic and issue covered. The publication is sold with the idea that the publisher is not required to render accounting, officially permitted, or otherwise, qualified services. If advice is necessary, legal or professional, a practiced individual in the profession should be ordered.

- From a Declaration of Principles which was accepted and approved equally by a Committee of the American Bar Association and a Committee of Publishers and Associations.

In no way is it legal to reproduce, duplicate, or transmit any part of this document in either electronic means or in printed format. Recording of this publication is strictly prohibited and any storage of this document is not allowed unless with written permission from the publisher. All rights reserved.

The information provided herein is stated to be truthful and consistent, in that any liability, in terms of inattention or otherwise, by any usage or abuse of any policies, processes, or directions contained within is the solitary and utter responsibility of the recipient reader. Under no circumstances will any legal responsibility or blame be held against the publisher for any reparation, damages, or monetary loss due to the information herein, either directly or indirectly.

Respective authors own all copyrights not held by the publisher.

The information herein is offered for informational purposes solely, and is universal as so. The presentation of the information is without contract or any type of guarantee assurance.

The trademarks that are used are without any consent, and the publication of the trademark is without permission or backing by the trademark owner. All trademarks and brands within this book are for clarifying purposes only and are the owned by the owners themselves, not affiliated with this document.

Table of Contents

Introduction 1

Chapter 1: Saint Lucia Awaits 5

Chapter 2: St. Lucia's Origins 9

Chapter 3: The Sights, The Sounds! 23

Chapter 4: Where to Stay? Hotels & Lodging 39

Chapter 5: Popular Cities 45

Chapter 6: Best Kept Secret Cities 53

Chapter 7: Travel Tips 61

Conclusion 71

Description 75

Introduction

Picture the perfect Caribbean getaway: quant fishing villages, reef diving, beautiful blue water home to reef diving adventures, and gorgeous volcanic beaches. Feel the warmth of the sun on your skin, the feel of the sand between your toes, and hear the waves as the break against the shore in the distance. Sounds almost too good to be true, right? If this sounds like your dream vacation, a trip to Saint Lucia might be just right for you!

Saint Lucia is a small Eastern Caribbean island located between Martinique and St. Vincent and the Grenadines. It is an island that has a large magnitude of adventures to offer you during your visit! The adventures awaiting you in Saint Lucia range from reef-diving off of the volcanic beaches to hiking through the rainforest to view stunning waterfalls. There are two cities in Saint Lucia that have much higher populations than the others; these cities are Castries and Soufriere. Castries and Soufriere are extremely popular vacation spots for tourists because of their size and the number of activities which they are able to offer vacationers. There are also multiple smaller, lesser known cities on the beautiful Caribbean island.

Some of Saint Lucia's smaller cities include Gros Islet, Canaries, and Dennery. While the smaller towns and cities of Saint Lucia may not be able to offer the hustle and bustle of shopping plazas or exciting night life, the smaller cities are often considered to be the island's hidden gems, which are home to gorgeous waterfalls, secluded beaches, and private getaway bed & breakfasts.

Not sure how to get to Saint Lucia? No worries! Many tourists choose to travel to the island by flying into the airport or by booking a cruise that makes it a point to visit the island during its travels. Worried that you do not know much about the history, culture, and features of Saint Lucia? Don't be! This travel guide can help you to learn about Saint Lucia's interesting history, discover the rich culture of the island, and evaluate the vast adventures awaiting you there! The chapters of this travel guide begin by walking you through a brief history of Saint Lucia, along with information about the island's geography, climate, and native wildlife. This travel guide then lists multiple options for where to stay while you are on your Caribbean vacation, as there are many available hotels and resorts in each city of Saint Lucia. The travel guide also explores some of the

Introduction

Caribbean island's best know cities, as well as the smaller, lesser known cities.

Hang on tight as we discover all that the beautiful and secluded island of Saint Lucia has to offer; you just may find that you have a difficult time leaving such a wonderous, relaxing place!

Chapter 1
Saint Lucia Awaits

Everyone's dream vacation is different. For some people, a dream vacation means shopping for hours in Paris. Another person's dream vacation could be spending hours laying in the sun on a beach in the Caribbean. Maybe you prefer educational and historical vacations in cities such as Washington DC or Boston.

What do you consider to be your dream vacation? Do you enjoy vacations filled with dining, nightlife, and shopping? Or maybe you would prefer a vacation filled with adventure: snorkeling, fishing, and hiking! Whichever vacation you personally prefer, you will be sure to experience it while visiting the beautiful island of Saint Lucia.

It can be easy to pass up the beautiful island of Saint Lucia as a vacation destination when you are trying to choose a new vacation spot. The name Saint Lucia itself does not sound extremely exciting, and sure there are more popular vacation destinations out there, such as Paris, Rome, New York, or Miami. Many of those who do visit Saint Lucia may not have planned to visit the island specifically as a part of their vacation plans; rather, they may find that the island is just one of many stops for their Caribbean cruise vacation.

Whether you are trying to plan a three-day vacation or three-week vacation, Saint Lucia has plenty of sights and activities to keep your whole vacation interesting. Saint Lucia can be a wonderful vacation on its own or a wonderful addition to a cruise vacation. Whether you are planning a family vacation or a solo getaway, make sure that you don't count Saint Lucia out just yet! This beautiful island is rich in heritage and culture that are sure to give you a relaxing, memorable vacation!

Be sure to plan your trip wisely so that you can experience as much of the beautiful island of Saint Lucia as possible. Saint Lucia has so much to offer to visitors, and it can be almost impossible to fit all of these experiences into a single trip. More than one of

Saint Lucia's friendly towns has a weekly festival on Fridays: these festivals range from fish fries to block parties, but they are always filled with food, music, dancing, and fun. The beautiful Caribbean island also offers visitors the chance to explore and appreciate nature with its many mountain hiking trails, volcanic summits, mud pools, sulfur springs, bays, and rivers. You can also learn more and get in touch with a whole new world under the water's surface of the Caribbean Sea by going snorkeling or diving to view the abundance of underwater plants and animals that thrive just off of Saint Lucia's shore.

When traveling to Saint Lucia (or any other new destination, really) it is always a great idea to learn more about the history and culture before you find yourself cluelessly emerged in it. This travel guide is a great start to learning more about the island's origins, history, heritage, and culture; but please do not forget that there are many available resources available to you, and you can never be too prepared. Be sure to pack a pair of sandals for the beach, and close-toed shoes for hiking up mountains or through the rainforests. Bring some light and breathable clothing because the island of Saint Lucia's climate stays hot year-round. However, it can also be a great idea to pack a light, waterproof jacket in case you do encounter rain while visiting this Caribbean island. Bring your camera because this island has so many beautiful scenic views that trying to explain them to your friends when you return home without photos will never be able to do the natural landscape of Saint Lucia justice.

Chapter 2
St. Lucia's Origins

Saint Lucia is a gorgeous Caribbean island that is a popular stop for various different cruise ships. The island of Saint Lucia is beautiful and proudly features various buildings as well as historic sites that pay tribute to the island's history, culture, and heritage. In order to truly appreciate these historic sites, you may first want to gain at least a basic understanding of the island's origins. Taking into account the island's vast history will certainly help you in order to develop a great understanding of their proud heritage and culture (you are sure to see fine examples of both Saint Lucian heritage and culture in various towns or cities throughout the island). Just like with anywhere else, the locals appreciate tourists who take an active interest in their history, as many of them are quite proud of not only where they came from in the past, but the progress that they have made since them. This island has come a long way since the 1600s, and the proud locals are continuously dedicated to the progression of the island while keeping their heritage intact.

The national flag of Saint Lucia changed a grand total of fourteen times between the years 1660 and 1814, the main cause of this frequent change being that European nations and the Caribs were continuously fighting over power of the beautiful island. Under the Treaty of Paris in 1814, Saint Lucia became a British controlled Crown colony. Under British control, the island of Saint Lucia became a thriving plantation economy that was largely based on the production of sugar. Enslaved African Americans were the island's predominant workers until slavery was abolished in Britain in the year 1834.

Until the year 1959, the island of Saint Lucia was a member of the Windward Islands Federation. In 1959, Saint Lucia switched from being a member of the Windward Islands Federation and instead joined the West Indies Federation, where it suggested that British countries in the Caribbean should be independent as a federation. Larger members of the West Indies Federation disagreed heavily, which eventually led to the dissolution of West Indies Federation in the year 1962, when the larger members did in fact seek independence.

In 1979, Saint Lucia finally became an independent member of the Commonwealth as well as a constitutional monarchy. John Compton served as Saint Lucia's first Prime Minister.

Today, Saint Lucia is still a member of the Commonwealth and it is the second largest member of the Windward group (also part of the Lesser Antilles). Saint Lucia has an overall island population of roughly 178,000, with roughly 70,000 of these people residing in the island's capital of Castries. Saint Lucia is one of the smallest countries in the world, though it is ranked in the top 50 for high population densities (roughly 298 people for each square kilometer). The people that call Saint Lucia home are predominantly African or of mixed African-European descent.

If you are considering visiting Saint Lucia for a vacation, it is important to know that the island's official language is English and 95% of the island's population fluently speak Lucian Creole French (natives refer to the language as Patwah).

Geography

The island of Saint Lucia is unique in that it is able to be home to a wide variety of different environments, ranging from tall mountain ranges and volcanic craters to white, sandy beaches and heavily shaded rainforests. Because the island is home to so many different environments, the island is also home to a wide variety of native wildlife (the biodiversity of the island will be discussed in a later section to more thoroughly cover the information). The island of Saint Lucia is located in the Caribbean Sea. Saint Lucia is roughly twenty-four miles (39km) south of the island of Martinique and roughly twenty-one miles (34km) northeast of the island of Saint Vincent. It is twenty-seven miles (43km) long with a maximum width of fourteen miles (23 km).

The island of Saint Lucia is formed predominantly of volcanic rock, and the island is home to the only "drive-in" volcano in the whole world. The island's volcano in Soufriere is locally known as the Sulphur Springs, but is a must-see part of the island's geography for anyone: natives and tourists alike! The Soufriere volcano has a road that runs not only up to the volcanic crater but runs through it as well, which gives tourists an up-close view of the volcano's steam and bubbling mud. While the Soufriere volcano on the island of Saint Lucia has not erupted since the 18th century and is considered to be dormant, there is another volcano featuring the same name, the Soufriere Hills Volcano that is located on the island of Montserrat that is still extremely active.

Saint Lucia is a beautiful island that is not only home to a volcano, but also to several mountains and rivers as well. It has dozens of streams that flow into multiple rivers, these rivers eventually flow to the sea. Saint Lucia's four largest rivers are the Soufriere, Mabouya, Cul de Sac, and Canelles. Saint Lucia's highest peak on the island is the mountain peak of Mount Gimie (measuring roughly 3,117'). The four largest mountains that can be found on the island of Saint Lucia are Gros Piton, Petit Piton, Qualibou, and Mount Gimie. The mountains allow water to drain through several fertile valleys before finally flowing into the much larger rivers of Saint Lucia.

Climate

Of the Windward Islands, Saint Lucia is the second largest. The island is home to beaches, broad valleys, rainforests, and mountain ranges, with the highest peak being Mount Gimie, measuring in at 3,117 feet (950m). The annual temperatures in Saint Lucia range from 70 degrees Fahrenheit (21 degrees Celsius) to 90 degrees Fahrenheit (32 degrees Celsius). The island experiences a fair amount of rainfall from June to November, while experiencing a much drier season between December and May. The beaches that can be found on the island's north can be very hot with the regular experience of trade winds to cool the temperature, while the interior of Saint Lucia is heavily rain forested, which can make the climate hotter and more humid. Saint Lucia is also affected by an annual hurricane season running from June to November.

Tropical Fruit & Exports

Because the Saint Lucian climate stays hot year-round, this island has the perfect environment for growing various tropical fruits. This Caribbean island has been producing a variety of tropical fruits for quite some time, and their food products are even one of the island's main exports to other countries. Some of the tropical fruits that are often grown on the island of Saint Lucia are nutmeg, soursop, and coconuts. In history, the main three exports to provide income for the island of Saint Lucia were cocoa, cotton, and tobacco. More recently the island became predominantly known for it's large sugar plantations, though that only lasted until the 1940's. After the 1940's, the island of Saint Lucia was focused on the production of bananas (a tropical fruit that can still be found in various places throughout the island).

Biodiversity

The natural wildlife that can be found living on the island of Saint Lucia is incredibly breathtaking, though many of these native species are critically endangered. Saint Lucia is an island that is home to many various types of snakes, lizards, mammals, and birds. The island is able to be the perfect native home to such a wide variety of species because the island has several very different types of environments ranging from dry mountain ranges to wet rainforest regions. Some of the snakes that are native to the island of Saint Lucia are the boa constrictor, the Saint Lucia racer, the Fer-de-lance, and the worm snake. Saint Lucia is also home to many species of geckos and lizards, including iguanas and the Saint Lucia Whiptail. Reptiles not really your style? Don't worry! The island is not only home to a wide variety of reptile species, but is home to a beautiful collection of birds in the trees as well. The bird species that the island of Saint Lucia is best known for is the Saint Lucia Amazon Parrot; these beautiful birds are blue, green, and red in color. Though beautiful, the Saint Lucia Amazon Parrot is in great danger, as an estimated 400-500 birds are all that remain of this species (this number is taken on a global scale). Some of the island's mammal species include the mongoose, the agouti, and the manicou. Below we have provided a brief summary of each of some of the native animals that are common to the tropical island of Saint Lucia.

<u>Saint Lucia Whiptail:</u> The male Saint Lucia Whiptail lizard is a visually appealing lizard that features the colors of the Saint Lucia national flag:

yellow, black, and blue. The Saint Lucia Whiptail lizards are roughly 10cm long and have an average weight of 30g. The lizard is native to the Caribbean island of Saint Lucia and currently has a status of being a Vulnerable (VU) species. The Saint Lucia Whiptail is most relaxed in an area of thick floral cover, making the dense forests of Saint Lucia the perfect home for these lizards. Its diet consists mostly of scorpions, insects, and fruit.

Saint Lucia Amazon Parrot: The Saint Lucia Amazon Parrot is the only parrot that is native to the Caribbean island of Saint Lucia. The Saint Lucia Amazon Parrot is beautifully colored with red, green, and blue feathers that stand out vibrantly in the sunlight (though the green does help them to stay hidden under the cover of their rainforest habitat).

This parrot tends to be a rather loud species that is capable of making a variety of different noises, which range from cackling to screeching. The parrot's diet consists largely of fruit and seeds which it gathers from the treetops of the Saint Lucian rainforests. The Saint Lucia Amazon Parrot tends to live pretty high up in treetops, with the average height of their nests being between 500 and 900 meters off the ground. Though the Saint Lucia Amazon Parrot is protected by domestic legislation, the bird is still listed as a vulnerable species.

Mongoose: The mongoose is a small, brown mammal that is native to the Caribbean island of Saint Lucia (among other places). This mammal can weigh up to eleven pounds and is a predatory animals that often resides in underground burrows. The diet of a mongoose consists of fruits, nuts, and seeds, as well as other small animals such as frogs, reptiles, birds, and rodents. Some mongoose species have even been

St. Lucia's Origins

known to bravely attack venomous snakes in order to consume them for a meal, an event that was featured in the fictional story *Rikki-tikki-tavi*. While mongoose seem to be thriving in areas which they are not native to (such as Hawaii, where they were introduced in an attempt to control the rodent problem inherent to sugarcane plantations), the mongoose species is considered to be threatened in its native areas, like Saint Lucia and Africa.

Agouti: The agouti is a mammal that is native to the Caribbean island of Saint Lucia as well as rainforests in Central and South America. This mammal is also a rodent, and at the first glance it looks a lot like a rather large guinea pig. The agouti has short, coarse, brown fur that is covered in a stinky oil that is used to act as a sort of natural raincoat. The agouti has sixteen toes total: five on each front foot, and three toes on each back foot. The agouti walks about on its toes rather than flatly on its feet like many other mammals and rodents. It appears to be tailless, but it does in fact have a very (very) short tail. Agoutis reside in hollow tree trunks or burrows, as these places allow them to stay safely hidden from large predators such as ocelots, coatimundis, and jaguars. The Agouti is able to jump up to an impressive six feet high, and its diet consists mainly of fruit, seeds, nuts, plants, and even crabs!

St. Lucia's Origins

Manicou: The manicou is what the locals of Saint Lucia call a common opossum. Though the opossums that are found on the island of Saint Lucia tend to be skinnier than American opossums, they have extremely similar diets and habits.

Chapter 3
The Sights, The Sounds!

You would have to try very hard to become bored on your vacation to the beautiful island of Saint Lucia (no really, you would actually have to make it a personal goal and put forth the effort necessary in order to become bored). The island of Saint Lucia has a seemingly endless list of activities and sights for you to enjoy during your visit. Below we have provided a list of the island's most popular activities so that you can be sure to fill your vacation with fun adventures from start to finish.

Climb Gros Piton

The large mountain of Gros Piton (as well as the smaller mountain Petit Piton) is located in the Saint Lucian city of Soufriere adjacent to the Soufriere Bay. The massive mountain of Gros Piton measures an amazing 798 meters in height, which makes it the second-tallest mountain in the country. Many tourists enjoy climbing the mountain of Gros Piton, and the mountain has become a very popular spot for tourists to enjoyable spend their day hiking while experiencing breathtaking views of the Soufriere Bay.

Sulphur Springs

The volcanic summit on the island of Saint Lucia is the only drive-in volcano in the whole world, so it is definitely not something that you should skip seeing while visiting Saint Lucia. While you want to be sure not to get too close, visitors can wander close to the volcanic summit in order to get a glimpse into the crater to see were the volcano's magma and heat meet. The Sulphur Springs create bubbling mud, smoke and ash. Keep in mind that the Sulphur Springs are too hot to bathe in though, as the spring temperatures can approach 200 degrees Celsius.

Sulphur Spring Mud Pools

Also located in the beautiful city of Soufriere are the Sulphur Spring Mud Pools. Because the Sulphur Springs are located on mountainous terrain, the water run downhill to create several different mud pools. These mud pools are very popular with locals and tourists alike because they have been proven to relieve skin disease, cure tension, and greatly reduce stress levels. The mud pools have accommodations that make them completely public friendly, with marked and separate changing rooms and showers. While visiting the beautiful island of Saint Lucia, be sure to enjoy a healing and relaxing mud bath!

Relax on Vigie Beach

Vigie beach is not your typical beach and for all of the best reasons! Here on Vigie beach, you will not find noisy crowds, huge beach umbrellas, or bulky plastic beach chairs. Instead you will find an abundance of fresh air, powdery white sand, cool breezes, and relaxation. Bring a prepared lunch, some sun screen, and a large beach towel in order to take full advantage of the natural beauty of Vigie Beach for the day. Spend the day sunbathing or the evening with a relaxing stroll on the beach. Either way you are sure to love this beautiful beach destination!

Experience History at Morne Fortune

Morne Fortune is a historic hill resting high above the capital city of Castries. This hill was home to some very intense fighting between the British and French colonies. The hill of Morne Fortune is home to an abundant amount of history that was vital to the establishment and independence of the island of Saint

Lucia. If you are looking to spend some of your vacation in a place where history meets beauty, then be sure to take a nature walk up Morne Fortune.

Enjoy the Natural Beauty of Marigot Bay

Perhaps the perfect place to unwind with a glass of wine on your Caribbean vacation is the beautiful location of Marigot Bay. Marigot Bay is a small inlet that is located between the city of Castries and the Canaries. This quant little bay is located just a short distance from George F.L. Charles Airport, so you can easily begin your dream vacation here. While visiting Marigot Bay you will be exposed to cool breezes, a beautiful bay, and dozens of sailboats. Marigot Bay is also the home of Marina Village; you can easily travel to a wide variety of shops, boutiques, and restaurants that will offer you the perfect relaxing way to begin your vacation.

Soufriere Estate Botanical Gardens

Located on the south-western end of the Saint Lucian island is the botanical gardens located on the Soufriere Estate. These botanical gardens are home to a variety of breathtakingly beautiful flowers, such as green ferns, deep red hibiscus, and large, waxy orchids. The paths that will lead you through the botanical gardens will lead you into well-kept jasmine and bamboo groves. The botanical gardens also offer a relaxing spa with hot pools that will help you to relive both tension and stress while on your vacation getaway. Once you have relaxed at the adjacent spa and viewed the multiple gorgeous flowers, be sure to view the Diamond Falls in the center of the gardens (these beautiful falls display water running elegantly over moss-covered rocks).

Enjoy Some Time at Treetop Adventure Park

Vacations are, of course, a great time to sit back and relax. After a few days of recovering from the hustle and bustle of everyday life by doing nothing, you may be ready to get your adrenaline pumping with an exciting experience. Treetop Adventure Park is a great place to feel the rush and excitement of treetop ziplining. Treetop Adventure Park has a dozen different ziplines available for guests to use (the longest zipline is 800ft, while the shortest is 83 ft.). If you are interested in spending some time at the Treetop Adventure Park, however, make sure that you are not afraid of heights (or at least be willing to conquer this fear for the sake of an unforgettable experience). The highest zipline cable at Treetop Adventure Park is 150ft high, which certainly contributes to the thrilling adrenaline that you will feel while cruising through the treetops of the Saint Lucian rainforest. Ready to experience treetop ziplining? All you will need to enjoy your time at Treetop Adventure Park is a pair of close-toed shoes and $65 (price is the same for adults and children).

Cool Off at Splash Island Water Park

Floating offshore of the Reduit Beach in southern Gros Islet is the water wonderland Splash Island Water Park. Splash Island Water Park is a great place for your kids to play and experience the warm Caribbean waters while running across inflatable islands. The Splash Island Water Park also includes a variety of obstacles, monkey bars, volley ball courts, walkways, and bounce houses to challenge your children as they find a place to truly enjoy your Caribbean vacation.

Spend Some Money at Castries Market

The Castries Market is located right within the heart of Saint Lucia's capital city of Castries. This outdoor marketplace features dozens of stands featuring friendly and smiling locals who have come out to offer tourists some of the island's best (and freshest) produce. While shopping at the Castries Market you will be able to purchase unbelievably fresh papayas, cucumbers, and plantains. The market in Castries also offers you the chance to purchase fresh (and extremely fragrant) spices, such as cinnamon and vanilla. If you are worried that you nearing the end of your vacation and fear that you cannot take some fresh produce back with you, you will still be able to purchase handmade trinkets, crafts, and souvenirs, which you can treasure for years to come!

Take a Hike! (Through the Rainforest)

The island of Saint Lucia is home to dozens of hiking trails that will allow you to experience the natural beauty of the Saint Lucian rainforests. The island's rainforests are home to a variety of wildlife, ranging from curious mammals and elusive reptiles to gorgeous tropical birds that call the treetops home. There are trails for everyone, whether you wish to take a leisurely walk through the rainforest or hike one of the many mountains that emerge from the treetops. Be sure to wear breathable clothing, as the temperatures can increase in both heat and humidity, and try to pack a light, waterproof jacket, if possible, just incase you experience some rainfall. Grab a few bottles of water and a small bottle of insect repellant, and you are on your way to enjoying the scenic beauty of the Saint Lucian rainforests (don't forget your camera)!

Weekend Culinary Creations

Block parties are an American tradition that some people grow up enjoying often, sometimes as often as once every few weeks. Saint Lucia has its own version of block parties, and these food festivals take place most weekends on the island. Locals come out to cook together, enjoy music, and take part in a great time to be had by all with story telling and dancing! Some of the common culinary features of these weekend food festivals are lobster, shrimp, Caribbean fish, and chilled beer. Even if you are not an experienced or dedicated foodie, you are sure to enjoy the increasingly positive vibe given off by the samba dancing and reggae music!

Get Your Buzz with Antilla Brewing Company

Saint Lucia is not home to an abundant variety of microbreweries, but there is one outstanding brewing company that is located just a short distance away from the Saint Lucia Cruise Ship Terminal in Gros Islet. The Antilla Brewing Company was established in the year of 2015 by an ambitious team of Canadians. This microbrewery is home to the restaurant trifecta:

comfortable environment, hand-crafted ales, and delicious food that will leave you feeling full and satisfied. The Antilla Brewing Company offers a variety of hand-crafted beers (such as their popular Golden Wheat and Stout), as well as a variety of delicious foods, ranging from burgers and hotdogs to spicy jerk wings and wedges. While you are here, you and your friends can ask for smaller glasses so that you can sample a greater variety of the hand-crafted beers in order to get a feel for which one is really your favorite. If you are looking for good people, good food, and good beer, then the Antilla Brewing Company is the place for you!

Visit Pigeon Island National Park

Pigeon Island National Park is located across from Rodney Bay and is perhaps one of the most important historic attractions on the beautiful island of Saint Lucia. While the control of Saint Lucia was still being continuously fought over, the hills of Pigeon Island National Park allowed for British settlers to carefully monitor the progressive movements of French troops. Pigeon Island National Park is a beautiful and scenic place for guests to hike to the top lookout points as well as view historic military buildings and the island's clean white beaches.

Dive at the Marine National Park of Anse Chastanet

The Anse Chastanet Marine National Park is home to a coral reef that offers divers the once in a lifetime chance to experience a large magnitude of sea life. In the shallow waters of the coral reef, divers can view and appreciate various corals and colored sponges. Brave enough to dive deeper? The deeper depths of the coral reef will open you up to the world of barracudas, parrotfish, goatfish, wrasse, and chromis. Feeling brave enough to dive deeper still? Don't dive too deep, but the coral reef features a plateau that drops off to a depth of 46 meters; these depths are home to a wide variety of eels, lobsters, and crabs. The beach at the Anse Chastanet Marine National Park is home to glorious views of the twin Pitons, while infinite beauty waits below the water's surface with the coral reef's biodiversity.

Visit Derek Walcott Square

Derek Walcott Square was named after a native of Saint Lucia and Nobel Laureate, Derek Walcott. Walcott was a playwright and poet who was awarded the Nobel Prize in Literature in the year of 1922. Derek Walcott worked at the University of Essex as a Professor of Poetry for three years between 2010 and 2013. Derek Walcott passed away in March of 2017; however, the Derek Walcott Square is still a popular spot to begin your vacation in Castries. The Derek Walcott Square is home to the Cathedral of Immaculate Conception, undoubtedly the square's most famous landmark. The center of the Derek Walcott Square features a large, beauty, Italian-style clock tower. The square is also home to the public library (restored) and beautifully historic colonial buildings with verandahs that shade the sidewalk below them.

Explore the Enbos Saut waterfall trail

In order to access and explore the Enbos Saut waterfall trail, you will have to arrive in Edmund (located above the city of Soufriere). The peak of Saint Lucia's highest mountain, Mount Gimie, is home to the Enbos Saut waterfall. Visitors can explore this trail to view the waterfall as well as breathtaking views of the Pitons by exploring a trail that takes an estimated 2.5 hours to complete. Well worth the walk, you will want to be sure that you are equipped with comfortable hiking shoes. As you explore the trail, you are likely to see a wide variety of avian life ranging from the Saint Lucia parrot to the Saint Lucia oriole (you also may view the Saint Lucia wren and Sempers warblers). If you are a classic gardener with a limited interest in birdwatching, you will also enjoy the exotic plant life that can be found along the trail: exotic plant life such as Honduras Mahogany and the Blue Mahoe.

Experience the "Stairway to Heaven"

The "Stairway to Heaven" is a well-known set of steps that leads hikers up to a breathtaking 360-degree view of the Saint Lucian countryside. The "Stairway to Heaven" is located on the Tet Paul Nature Trail, and it takes roughly 45 minutes to complete. The trail itself is rated as being beginner friendly while still allowing guests to view exotic tropical fruits as well as medicinal trees and plants.

Chapter 4
Where to Stay? Hotels & Lodging

Anse Chastanet

Anse Chastanet is a gorgeous resort that is sure to help you get in touch with your romantic side. This beautiful, intimate resort is perfect for weddings, honeymoons, or romantic getaways. Anse Chastanet is located on a gorgeous 600-acre property near Soufriere. The property itself is quiet and private. The resort staff are caring and help to ensure that your romantic getaway will be filled with all of the classic memories that it should have. The Anse Chastanet resort also has a long list of activities to keep you busy and allow you to experience new things throughout your stay. Just a few of the numerous activities which you can participate in during your time at the Anse Chastanet are the chocolate lab, jungle biking, bird watching, yoga, spa treatments, and a fine dining treehouse restaurant! Voted the most romantic resort in the Caribbean, you and your significant other are sure to love reconnecting at this beautiful and scenic resort!

Jade Mountain Resort

Jade Mountain is an incredibly beautiful resort located in the bustling city of Soufriere. Though the resort does not offer internet or television, it is impossible to feel as though you are missing out on much while you experience its natural beauty. This unique resort offers rooms in which there are only three walls, the space where the fourth wall would be located is left open to accommodate 24 hour viewing of the Pitons as well as the Caribbean Sea. Jade Mountain is not limited to cozy rooms and mystical views, as the resort also offers a variety of activities to fill your days with excitement; these activities range from yacht sailing to snorkeling.

The Capella Marigot Bay

The Capella Marigot Bay is the perfect resort for you if you would prefer to spend your nights winding down from a busy day, away from noisy crowds of tourists. The Capella is relatively secluded, with few nearby attractions. While the resort's location is not ideal for walking to all of your favorite activities, it is one of the best resorts in which to experience a truly private and quiet evening relaxing near the Caribbean. The resort offers two large pools to the guests who seek peace here, and one of the large pools is built with an infinity edge that looks over the Marigot Bay. This resort is truly the perfect place for relaxation with its luxurious spa, freshwater pools, and secluded location. If you want to have a busy day in the cities, the resort staff will help you to arrange adequate transportation to and from the resort. If you wake up feeling like you just need a "do nothing day" that does not include a long walk to the beach, you can enjoy various massages and facials with the resort's spa before floating lazily in one of its large pools.

The Landings at Saint Lucia

Located in scenic Rodney Bay, the Landings at Saint Lucia offers its guests an amazing stay in the fully equipped suites that guests have said feel more like apartments than your traditional hotel room. This hotel sits right on the beach so that you can experience fun activities such as sunbathing, scuba diving, sailing, or snorkeling anytime you want! The hotel also features three restaurants so that you can experience and enjoy a wide variety of cuisine without even having to leave the hotel. This hotel is centered in an area where natural beauty is abundant, as the hotel rooms feature breathtaking ocean and mountain views.

Auberge Seraphine

If you are looking for private and bright accommodations without have to fight for a beachfront reservation, then the hotel Auberge Seraphine located in Castries may be perfect for you! This hotel offers its guests bright and colorful rooms that also include a water view (all of the rooms with the exception of six offer a water view). This hotel may not feature some of the special accommodations that can be expected from larger resorts, but the hotel does have excellent convenience to the nearby airport as well as downtown Castries and many wonderful restaurants. This hotel also provides its guests with an in-house restaurant, complimentary free Wi-Fi, and a large pool.

Bay Gardens Beach Resort and Spa

This beautiful resort and spa is located in Rodney Bay right on the Reduit Beach. This luxurious resort features a lagoon style pool for it's guests; it will help anyone stay cool and relaxed while on their Caribbean vacation. Each of the suites at the Bay Gardens Beach Resort and Spa are fully equipped with dining and kitchen areas. The resort is also located very conveniently near several different spas, restaurants, and tourist activities. This resort also comes with complimentary free Wi-Fi for its guests. Being located on the best beach in Saint Lucia as well as near a wide variety of activities and restaurants, this beach resort and spa is extremely popular, so be sure to book your reservation ahead of time!

Chapter 5
Popular Cities

Castries

Castries is the capital of the Caribbean island of Saint Lucia, and while it may not have an abundance to offer in the historical sites category, the city is well worth a stop, if not for its scenery alone.

Many of the city's historic buildings were completely destroyed in various major fires that took place between the years 1785 and 1945; however, the city is still extremely popular due to it's scenic natural beauty. The main natural attraction of Castries is no doubt the mountain of Morne Fortune, which reaches heights of almost 3,000 feet tall.

Castries is located near the George F.L. Charles Airport, so this city is a common spot for thousands of tourists to officially begin their Caribbean island vacation. There are several restaurants located within the busy streets of Castries that are well known for their delicious and authentic island cuisines (these restaurants serve a variety of food options ranging from Creole to Caribbean food choices). Two of the most common tourist stops within Castries are the Derek Walcott

Market (named for Saint Lucian native Nobel Laureate Derek Walcott) and the Castries Market, where natives sell a variety of fresh fruit, spices, crafts, and souvenirs. The Derek Walcott Square is home to the Cathedral of the Immaculate Conception, undoubtedly the square's most famous landmark. The center of Derek Walcott Square features a large, beautiful, Italian-style clock tower. The square is also home to the public library (restored) and beautiful, historic, colonial buildings with verandahs that shade the sidewalk below them.

The Castries Market is located right within the heart of Saint Lucia's capital city of Castries. This outdoor marketplace features dozens of stands featuring friendly and smiling locals who have come out to offer tourists some of the island's best (and freshest) produce. While shopping at the Castries Market, you will be able to purchase unbelievably fresh papayas, cucumbers, and plantains. The market in Castries also offers you the chance to purchase fresh (and extremely fragrant) spices, such as cinnamon and vanilla.

Morne Fortune is a historic hill resting high above the capital city of Castries. This hill was home to some very intense fighting between the British and French colonies. The hill of Morne Fortune is home to an abundant amount of history that was vital to the establishment and independence of the island of Saint Lucia. If you are looking to spend multiple fun filled days in Castries, then you can also try catamaran sailing and helicopter tours. Castries is a bustling but beautiful city that should be on the "must see" list of any Caribbean vacationer!

Vieux Fort

Vieux Fort was once the capital of Saint Lucia before Castries was named the new capital for the island. Vieux Fort is located roughly twenty miles south of Castries and overlooks the scenic views of Vieux Fort Bay. The city of Vieux Fort is not as large as Castries, though it is enjoyed by many for its clean, sandy beaches that offer the ideal environment for sunbathing, swimming, and snorkeling.

Micoud

The city of Micoud in Saint Lucia is located adjacent to Vieux Fort and thus offers tourists its own collection of beautiful beaches on the Caribbean Sea. One of the most popular places to visit while in Micoud is the Latille Waterfalls and Gardens. The Latille Waterfalls and Gardens are said to be very easy for tourists to find, this search made easier by many friendly locals who are frequently coming to and from the falls. The Latille Waterfalls and Gardens have several small pools with very small fish that will even give you a natural Caribbean pedicure by removing the dead skin from your feet. These natural pedicures are great for your skin. Simply dip your feet in the cool pool of water and wait! The Latille Waterfalls and Gardens are also home to a beautiful waterfall that tourists can stand under as a sort of natural shower. They can also swim in the clear pool of water collected at the base of the falls. The Latille Waterfalls and Gardens are shaded over with a sort of jungle environment, making this location a great spot for guests to escape the heat and enjoy the cool breeze supplied by nature.

Soufriere

While Castries may be the capital of Saint Lucia, Soufriere is a close second when it comes to ranking the island's cities to determine tourist favorites (some may even rank it as number one). Soufriere is home to the great twin mountains Gros Piton and Petit Piton, beautiful natural mountains that visitors can hike up to experience breathtaking panoramic views of the island. Soufriere is the perfect destination if you would like to visit a location that has been able to perfectly blend city and rainforest environments.

Located on the south-western end of the Saint Lucian island is the botanical gardens, on the Soufriere Estate. These botanical gardens are home to a variety of breathtakingly beautiful flowers such as green ferns, deep red hibiscus, and large, waxy orchids. The paths that will lead you through the botanical gardens will lead you into well-kept jasmine and bamboo groves. The botanical gardens also offer a relaxing spa with hot pools that will help you to relieve both tension and stress while on your vacation getaway. Once you have relaxed at the adjacent spa and viewed the multiple gorgeous flowers, be sure to view the Diamond Falls in the center of the gardens (these beautiful falls display water running elegantly over moss-covered rocks).

The large mountain of Gros Piton (as well as the smaller mountain Petit Piton) is located in the Saint Lucian city of Soufriere adjacent to the Soufriere Bay. The massive mountain of Gros Piton measures an amazing 798 meters in height, which makes it the second-tallest mountain in the country. Many tourists enjoy climbing the mountain of Gros Piton, and it has become a very popular spot for tourists to enjoyably spend their day hiking while experiencing breathtaking views of the Soufriere Bay. Soufriere is also home to

Marigot Bay, Pigeon Island National Park, Reduit Beach, and the Sulphur Springs. So, whether your dream vacation is to lounge on the beach or spend the day immersed in local shops and culture, Soufriere has something great to offer everyone who visits!

Chapter 6
Best Kept Secret Cities

Dennery

If you are visiting Saint Lucia for a few days or maybe even multiple weeks, you should make sure to spare some time to spend exploring the natural beauty surrounding the small town of Dennery. Dennery can be an often-overlooked tourist town, but that just means you will not have to worry about large and noisy crowds during your visit. While Dennery may not be home to the wide variety of shops and restaurants that the larger cities are able to offer, this city is home to a variety of parks, botanical gardens, and gorgeous waterfalls that will make anyone appreciate the true beauty of nature.

The small city of Dennery is located within the Mabouya Valley. Leading to it is an abundance of waterfalls, natural parks, and scenic hiking trails. If you are an individual who enjoys feeling close to nature, you may very well enjoy the Barre de l'Isle Forest Reserve, which is a nature preserve that can be found just four and a half miles west of Dennery. This nature preserve will allow you the chance to hike trails that wind through the forest and up the mountain. Stay on alert and you should be able to see a variety of Saint Lucia's wildlife.

Dennery is also known for the beautiful waterfalls which it is home to, and there are two waterfalls that are of particular interest to visitors. The first waterfall that is definitely worth your time in Dennery is La Tille Waterfall. The waterfall is located six miles south of Dennery. La Tille Waterfall is located within a nature park with beautiful gardens, while the waterfall itself gives visitors the chance to stand under the falling water while swimming in a naturally created pool at the base of the waterfall.

The second waterfall that is well known and appreciated in Dennery is the Sault Falls. These waterfalls are located a short mile west of Dennery. While the Sault Falls are one of the larger waterfalls on the island of Saint Lucia, they do not receive the publicity they deserve, which means you won't have to stand in a crowd to appreciate their beauty.

If you enjoy beautiful botanical gardens, you, may wish to visit the Mamiku Gardens (3 miles south of Dennery) or the King George V Gardens. Both gardens offer a wide variety of beautiful plant life that will leave you feeling relaxed.

Gros Islet

Gros Islet is a smaller town on the island of Saint Lucia. It may not be the best hot spot for tourist activities, but Gros Islet does have something to offer that the other cities do not: a weekly Friday night street party. The Friday night street party that occurs each week in Gros Islet is the longest running street party on the island of Saint Lucia. Locals come together each week for this huge street party to grill chicken, seafood, and pork on large barbeque grills. The street party features music from local artists and DJ's that provide the perfect party atmosphere for dancing.

Gros Islet is the perfect place for young couples who want to add a bit of partying to their vacations.

Saint Lucia is not home to an abundant variety of microbreweries, but there is one outstanding brewery that is located just a short distance away from the Saint Lucia Cruise Ship Terminal in Gros Islet. The Antilla Brewing Company was established in the year of 2015 by an ambitious team of Canadians.

Floating offshore of the Reduit Beach in southern Gros Islet is the water wonderland Splash Island Water Park. Splash Island Water Park is a great place for your kids to play and experience the warm Caribbean waters while running across inflatable islands. The Splash Island Water Park also includes a variety of obstacles, monkey bars, volley ball courts, walkways, and bounce houses to challenge your children as they find a place to truly enjoy your Caribbean vacation.

Praslin

Praslin is the area of Saint Lucia that sits snugly between Micoud and Dennery. Praslin is best known to tourists who enjoy taking the occasional adventure, as it is home to numerous beautiful and scenic hiking trails. While Praslin may not be able to offer you a day of partying or exciting night life, Praslin has many gorgeous natural features. After a long day of exploring and enjoying the natural beauty of the island, you are surely going to want a comfortable place to spend your night. If you want to spend an evening somewhere peaceful and quaint, you may be interested in one of the several bed and breakfasts that are located in Praslin. Praslin's bed and breakfasts, such as the A Peace of Paradise bed and breakfast, offer a refreshing change from the large and bustling resorts that make up the primary lodging options of the larger cities like Castries or Soufriere.

Canaries

The town of Canaries is a small fishing village located on Saint Lucia's western coast. This small town is hidden among the hills of Saint Lucia but offers visitors a colorful and peaceful look at some of the island's traditional culture. Though the fishing industry is not as predominant as it had once been, it is still a vital way of life to the people of Canaries. It is one way that they hold onto their culture, traditions, and heritage, in addition to providing food. Visitors to the small town of Canaries can see dozens of small and colorful fishing boats docked in the bay.

The local name for this quaint fishing village is Kanawe, which means *cooking pots* in Amerindian. This word for the village is still highly applicable today, as represented in the large cauldrons that many Saint Lucians use for cooking in both their homes and businesses.

Canaries is set on a beautiful bay that is picture perfect for many, and a walk through this town will give you an insight to the island's past, history, culture, and heritage. Unlike the larger towns like Castries and Soufriere, Canaries seems to have hung back a bit when it comes to progression, as they still show strong acknowledgements to their roots in daily life.

If you enjoy places that retain historic charm and a slower, simpler pace of life, then a visit to Canaries may be just what you need in your Caribbean vacation.

Anse La Raye

Anse La Raye is a gorgeous, traditional village located on the island of Saint Lucia. Perhaps the most prominent and popular building in Anse La Raye is the Roman Catholic Church (which has been in place on the island since the 1700s). Anse La Raye is the perfect vacation spot in order to fulfill any of your vacation needs as the town offers history, shopping, dining, diving, and a weekly nightlife celebration. You can also be sure to enjoy the Caribbean Sea while visiting Anse La Raye by swimming, sunbathing, fishing, or even tikaye diving.

Looking for a party scene or some upbeat night life while on your Caribbean vacation? Anse La Raye has a weekly Fish Fry Fiesta every Friday night, where locals prepare freshly caught fish to create the perfect variety of Caribbean cuisine to match the locally provided Caribbean music. You won't be able to resist eating, drinking, and dancing to your heart's content.

A great many of the buildings still standing today in Anse La Raye are over 100 years old and serve as fine examples of aged English and French architecture.

There is such a wide variety of cities on St. Lucia that everyone in your vacation crew, even the pickiest members, will find something to enjoy and cherish.

Chapter 7
Travel Tips

Just like with any vacation spot, there are many available travel tips for when you are enjoying your vacation on the beautiful Caribbean island of Saint Lucia. Unfortunately, you usually do not know about certain travel tips for a specific vacation spot unless you have already traveled there once (and usually made the mistakes yourself). In order to save you some frustration, time, and possibly money, we have provided several travel tips below to try and help your vacation to Saint Lucia be as enjoyable and stress-free as possible.

Use a Car Service

There are numerous travel websites that tell you that it is best for you to have a driver or taxi service pick you up at the airport to help you get around, and they are absolutely correct! The roadways in Saint Lucia are very different from those which you may be accustomed to, and it is very easy to get turned around on unfamiliar roadways. If you have a driver or taxi service pick you up, you will be able to sit back, relax, and enjoy the ride. Literally, they know where you want to go even if you are not quite sure. Having a car pick you up rather than renting a car to drive yourself around can help to avoid a lot of stress. Remember that you are on vacation. Relax and let someone else do the driving.

Bug Spray: It's A Thing, Use It!

Saint Lucia's climate is very hot and also very dry for the majority of the year. The mosquito problem in Saint Lucia is very real and applies to the whole island. Be sure to pack plenty of insect repellant with you for your vacation to Saint Lucia, and be sure to spray yourself with the repellant before leaving your hotel room. Also, do not forget to reapply the insect repellant after you take a swim, as many insect repellants are not waterproof or may be weakened when exposed to water.

If you are averse to some of the chemical sprays marketed today, you can use some essential oils as a homeopathic bug spray.

There are many great souvenirs that you will want to bring home with you from the Caribbean island of Saint Lucia, but mosquito bites are definitely not one of them.

Utilize Rodney Bay's Bike Rentals

If you are staying in Rodney Bay for even a small portion of your vacation to Saint Lucia it is of vital importance that you make a point to visit Pigeon Island. This beautiful island has breathtaking views of the surrounding Saint Lucian landscape that you will never forget (especially if you bring your camera). The walk to Pigeon Island may leave you slightly fatigued, which can affect your level of enjoyment once you finally arrive at your destination. Renting bikes is a great way to get to Pigeon Island at a faster speed, which will leave you more time in your day to view other surrounding areas of interest.

Visit the Free Sulphur Springs to Save Money

The Sulphur Springs on the island of Saint Lucia are one of the most popular attractions there because they are not something that you are able to see just anywhere. The entrance to the Sulphur Springs and mud baths in Soufriere is an average $5.00 USD per person; however there is a travel tip that will allow you to visit these Sulphur Springs as many times as you would like for free. Many of the locals swear by this little short cut, though they do not advertise the free route to tourists. It's sort of an island best-kept secret.

In order to access the Sulphur Springs for free, you will want to head down the steps to view the waterfall (be sure to do this BEFORE you are asked to pay an entrance fee to see the volcano). At the bottom of the steps near the waterfall, there is a Sulphur Spring that you will be able to visit as many times as you would like for free.

Make Friends with The Locals, Especially Boat Owners

Many of the island's most popular attractions and activities can be experienced for a fraction of the price if you are able to make friends with some of the island's locals who have access to the same services. For example, on Hummingbird Beach (located in Soufriere), there are multiple advertised boat excursions for tourists, though some of these guided tours can be on the pricey side. On Hummingbird Beach, however, there are also several local boat owners who are more than willing to take tourists on a private tour for a much lower price. Some of these private tours can be by locals have the added benefit of not being as strict on time, and the locals who are nice enough to offer these tours are often very knowledgeable and proud of the island of Saint Lucia itself.

*Note: *While you certainly can get better deals by taking unadvertised tours with friendly locals, it is still vitally important that you use your best judgement so as not to end up in a potentially dangerous situation while on your Caribbean island getaway.*

Try Not to Limit Yourself to Restaurants

While you are visiting the Caribbean island of Saint Lucia, you are sure to come across dozens of different options for where to get some delicious food as well as popular island cuisine. Some of the best Caribbean cuisine that you will have the opportunity to experience while vacationing on the island of Saint Lucia does not come from restaurants, but rather from roadside stands or food stalls that have been set up by native Saint Lucians. These native people local to the island offer the sale of fish that have been freshly caught off the island's coasts. The seafood dishes that the locals offer can be prepared a number of different ways, so you may want to try more than one in order to truly experience Caribbean cuisine. These delicious roadside food stands often offer the same Caribbean cuisine that you can purchase from restaurants, but with a few added benefits: the food is always fresh and usually cheaper than what is served at a restaurant. These

Caribbean cuisine roadside stands are scattered around the island of Saint Lucia, and many of them can be found in the cities of Gros Islet, Soufriere, and Canaries.

Be Smart About Avoiding Sunburn

Because Saint Lucia is located close to the equator, the effects of the sun are much stronger on this Caribbean island than for most of our hometowns located father away from the equator. Be cautious of the sun's rays so that you can avoid bringing home an unwanted and painful souvenir: sunburn. Wearing pants and long-sleeved shirts can help to greatly reduce your exposure to the direct sunlight, though the island's temperatures are generally very hot. Be sure that these are light clothing choices, as well.

Wearing a hat while on the island is a great idea and can not only help to reduce the chances of getting sunburn on your scalp. Wearing a hat will also help to keep the sun's bright rays out of your eyes as you try to enjoy your Caribbean vacation. While part of the enjoyment of vacationing on a Caribbean island such as Saint Lucia is the abundance of sunlight, you may want to seek shade when possible so that you are not exposing yourself to higher risks of sunburn, heat stroke, or dehydration.

One last tip for avoiding sunburn: use sunblock, and lots of it! Sunblock is a wonderful way for you to save your skin from being burned by the sun's harmful rays. Be sure to apply sunblock generously and reapply the sunblock every few hours as needed so that you receive maximum protection to avoid sunburn.

Watch for Snakes

There is only one poisonous snake that is native to the island of Saint Lucia, and that snake is the Fer-de-Lance. This snake has a wide triangular head that is much larger than its neck and the width of its body. The snake is brown or black and has light yellow bands that create a crisscrossing pattern across its body. The snake avoids any contact with humans, so your chances of accidentally happening upon one are pretty slim. In any case, be sure to watch your step when you go hiking and make sure that you can visually see the surface of a rock before you stick your hand out to touch the surface. If you do happen upon a Fer-de-Lance, they have been known to make a pretty significant amount of noise as a warning that you are too close. This noise is usually enough warning for you to reevaluate your surroundings and avoid that area.

Crime Exists Everywhere

Sadly, there have been more than just a few instances of people being robbed, assaulted, or otherwise taken advantage of while they were trying to enjoy a nice vacation away from home. While we are on vacation, we are trying to relax and live our lives in a carefree manner so as to finally relieve ourselves from the stresses that we can experience with daily life. You do not need to be paranoid or overly cautious while on vacation, as this can ruin the experience altogether, though it is important that you remain aware of your surroundings and be cautious. Make sure that you do not leave any personal belongings lying about (in a taxi, on a restaurant table, etc.) and make sure that you always keep an eye on those individuals who are around you.

Pick-pocketing is a very real problem in many of the more crowded tourist areas, so it may be a good idea to put your money into separate pockets. Place some of your money in a front pocket of your pants, some in a back pocket, and the rest in a backpack or purse. With your money separated, a crafty thief will not be able to steal all of it before they are noticed. By separating your money, you ensure that even if a thief does manage to steal your backpack or the money from your back pocket, you will still have other compartments containing money so that you do not find yourself penniless while on vacation.

Purchasing "Off Limits" Souvenirs

When you get off of the cruise ship or plane on the Caribbean island of Saint Lucia, you will almost certainly be approached by local vendors who are hoping that you will further contribute to the Saint Lucian economy by purchasing a variety of souvenirs from them. Some of these souvenirs are nice representations of the island but will likely not be able to make it home with you. Souvenirs that have been made from coconut husks or palm fronds will most likely be confiscated by customs because they are considered to be vegetation that has been removed from the island. There are also a few individuals on Saint Lucia (and we are sure that this is a problem almost anywhere) that may approach you and ask you if you would like to purchase drugs; obviously, say no and keep moving.

If a vendor seems to be excessively pushy or aggressive, make sure that you firmly tell them that you are not interested in what they are selling and keep moving. Vendors will always ask if you would like to purchase their products, and for most vendors a simple "No, thank you" is enough to show them that you are not interested in anything that they have to sell. Some vendors, however, can be pushier with their sales tactics. In this event, restate that you are not interested in a firm but nonaggressive voice. It is also vitally important in these situations that you keep moving, because stopping to restate your disinterest may only cause the situation to escalate.

You want to have a safe and enjoyable vacation, so make sure that you are always following these travel tips and using common sense. Follow these tips and use your head so that you will have a stress-free and safe vacation on the beautiful Caribbean island of Saint Lucia.

Conclusion

Vacations are a common tradition for most families. Maybe you are looking to find the perfect vacation destination because you simply need a place to get away. Whatever your reasons for wanting to enjoy a vacation, the first and most important step in planning it is choosing where you would like to visit. Choosing a vacation destination can be difficult because there are so many options. Would you want to vacation somewhere exciting and busy like New York City or Paris? Or perhaps somewhere more secluded and relaxing like Hawaii or Jamaica? Maybe you would most enjoy a vacation filled with music, dancing, and exciting nightlife. Or, are you one who is more at home enjoying nature's beauty on a beach or gorgeous forest hike? What if you didn't have to choose? What if there was a vacation destination where you could experience it all?

If you visit Saint Lucia, you can fill your vacation with thrills as well as lazy moments. Saint Lucia has an almost unlimited list of experiences to offer to you that range from scuba diving to sunbathing on the beach, and ziplining to shopping in quaint fishing villages. Discovering the natural beauty of this

Caribbean island is an experience that everyone should take part of once in their lifetime, though exploring all that the island has to offer can take longer than your standard family vacation will allow. Be sure to plan your trip wisely so that you are able to get the full experience of the fun, beauty, and wonder that Saint Lucia has to offer.

While planning your vacation, remember that Saint Lucia has a wide variety of activities and something for everyone to enjoy. If you enjoy outdoor activities, then you are sure to love Saint Lucia's volcanic crater, therapeutic mud pools, Sulphur springs, rainforests, glistening bays, and sandy beaches. If you would rather take part in exciting activities, you will surely enjoy the island of Saint Lucia's Caribbean cuisine, local music, nightlife, and shopping. Also keep in mind that for every dreamlike place that a vacation destination has to offer, there may be a negative individual or location elsewhere nearby. Remember to use common sense and keep your safety as a priority so that you have a truly enjoyable Caribbean vacation.

You know now of Saint Lucia's origins and have a brief understanding of the island's geography, climate, and natural wildlife. You know of the most popular

Conclusion

activities, sites, restaurants, hotels, and resorts. So, what are you waiting for?! Grab your shoes, pack a suitcase, and don't forget your camera! The gorgeous, peaceful Caribbean island of Saint Lucia is waiting for you to experience its beauty and charm!

Description

Picture the perfect Caribbean getaway: quaint fishing villages, reef diving, beautiful blue water home to reef diving adventures, and gorgeous volcanic beaches. Feel the warmth of the sun on your skin, the feel of the sand between your toes, and hear the waves as they break against the shore in the distance. Sounds almost too good to be true, right? If this sounds like your dream vacation, a trip to Saint Lucia might be just right for you!

Not sure how to get to Saint Lucia? No worries! Many tourists choose to travel to the island by flying into Saint Lucia airport or by booking a cruise that makes it a point to visit the island during its travels. Worried that you do not know much about the history, culture, and features of Saint Lucia? Don't be! This travel guide can help you to learn about the island's interesting history, discover the rich culture of the small nation, and evaluate the vast adventures awaiting you there! The chapters of this travel guide begin by walking you through a brief history of Saint Lucia, along with information about the island's geography, climate, and native wildlife. This travel guide then lists multiple options for where to stay while you are on your Caribbean vacation, as there are many available hotels and resorts in each city of Saint Lucia. The travel guide also explores some of the Caribbean island's best-known cities, as well as the smaller, less known cities.

Vacation is not always problem-free, so this travel guide also features numerous travel tips from those who have visited the Caribbean island of Saint Lucia multiple times. These travel tips are designed to make sure that your island vacation is stress-free, fun, exciting, and above all, safe. After you have read this travel guide for the information about the island of Saint Lucia, it is a good idea to hang onto it to refer to just before or even during your trip. You can never be too prepared, and this preparation will be a great help in avoiding any mishaps during your Caribbean getaway.

If you visit Saint Lucia, you can fill your vacation with thrills as well as lazy moments. Saint Lucia has an almost unlimited list of experiences to offer to you that range from scuba diving to sunbathing on the beach, and ziplining to shopping in quaint fishing villages. You will soon forget what day of the week it is, and your humdrum, work-a-day life back home will seem like a distant memory. You won't want to leave! You may find that you enjoy Saint Lucia so much that you visit it over and over again.

Hang on tight as we discover all that the beautiful and secluded island of Saint Lucia has to offer; you just may find that you have a difficult time leaving such a wonderous, relaxing place!

This travel guide will give you everything you need to know about a wonderful country – where to stay, where to visit, the history and more. If you want to know more about the country, download this guide and find out!

Printed in Great Britain
by Amazon